risotto

risotto

30 simply delicious vegetarian
recipes from an Italian kitchen

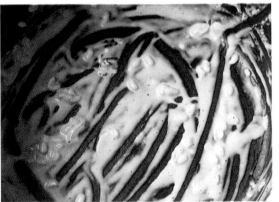

URSULA FERRIGNO

photography by Jason Lowe

RYLAND
PETERS
& SMALL

LONDON NEW YORK

SENIOR DESIGNER	Ashley Western
COMMISSIONING EDITOR	Elsa Petersen-Schepelern
EDITOR	Maddalena Bastianelli
PRODUCTION	Patricia Harrington
ART DIRECTOR	Gabriella Le Grazie
PUBLISHING DIRECTOR	Alison Starling
FOOD STYLIST	Ursula Ferrigno
COOKING ASSISTANT	Katherine McGhie
STYLIST	Rebecca Duke

AUTHOR'S ACKNOWLEDGEMENTS:
A big thank you to Katherine McGhie for her constant support and
assistance, and for being such a perfectionist; and to Kate O'Donnell,
for her utter professionalism and speedy typing. Thanks to the team
at Ryland Peters & Small, especially my editor, Maddie, for her
attention to detail, and for being such fun at the shoots; to Ashley for
designing such a gorgeous book; and to Elsa who invited me to write
it. To Jason, thanks for such beautiful photographs and for all the
laughs we shared. Finally, a special thank you to Antonio Carluccio
for his generosity with truffles. Many varieties of mushroom and
truffle are available from his store at 28a Neal Street, Covent Garden,
London, WC2H 9PS.

NOTES:
All spoon measurements are level unless otherwise stated.
Vialone nano is, in my opinion, the best risotto rice. Use this
variety if you can, otherwise use carnaroli or arborio instead.

First published in the United Kingdom in 2001
by Ryland Peters & Small
20–21 Jockey's Fields, London WC1R 4BW

10 9 8 7 6 5

Text © Ursula Ferrigno 2001
Design and photographs © Ryland Peters & Small 2001

ISBN 1 84172 111 5

A catalogue record for this book is available from the British Library.

Printed and bound in China by Toppan Printing Co.

introduction

Italians adore their pasta, but they also love risotto. Throughout Italy, and especially in the north, rice forms a large part of the nation's diet – probably because the dishes are quick to prepare, nutritious, inexpensive and addictively delicious. They are also very versatile – perfect for relaxed, weekday meals or smart dinner parties.

Risotto is made with short-grain rice, which absorbs a large amount of liquid without the grains losing their bite. There are three main varieties: arborio, carnaroli and vialone nano. Each one brings a slightly different texture to the dish. Arborio, perhaps the best-known, produces a dense risotto that can become too stiff if overcooked. Carnaroli is the most expensive, but its tender yet firm grain is ideal for risotto. It is also the least likely to overcook. Vialone nano is favoured by Venetian cooks and I think it is the best rice. It gives a creamy, voluptuous risotto. Italian delis and an increasing number of supermarkets now sell a good range of risotto rice.

Perfect risotto is easy to achieve. All you need is a good-quality risotto rice; home-made stock; a wide, shallow pan; and 18–20 minutes of constant stirring while the rice cooks. There are no short cuts.

Good risotto is made in stages. The key is to add hot, flavourful stock – a ladleful at a time – to the rice in the pan, stirring constantly until all the liquid has been absorbed and the rice is tender but still firm (*al dente*). It should never be dry or sticky, but have a 'wave-like' (*all'onda*) consistency. A risotto should stand for 2 minutes before serving, then be spooned into warmed bowls, not plates, and served with a fork, never a spoon.

The recipes in this book have been gathered over years of eating out in Italy – many are family recipes given to me by friends. If the vegetables I've suggested are not available, use whatever you can find fresh in the market.

Risotto in four easy steps

Top left: Lightly cook shallots in oil and butter until softened.

Top right: Add rice and stir until well coated and glistening.

Bottom left: Add stock, a ladleful at a time, and simmer, stirring until absorbed before adding more. Repeat until all the liquid has been absorbed and the rice is tender but still firm.

Bottom right: Mix in flavourings, such as vegetables, herbs and cheese.

Vegetable Stock

BRODO DI VERDURA

HOME-MADE STOCK (*BRODO*) IS ESSENTIAL WHEN MAKING RISOTTO. IT WILL GIVE THE BEST FLAVOUR. MAKE A BASIC STOCK WITH WHATEVER FRESH VEGETABLES ARE AVAILABLE, THEN REFRIGERATE OR FREEZE UNTIL NEEDED.

40 g unsalted butter
1 tablespoon olive oil
3 garlic cloves, crushed
1 large onion, coarsely chopped
4 leeks, washed and coarsely chopped
2 carrots, coarsely chopped
2 celery stalks, coarsely chopped
1 fennel bulb, coarsely chopped
a handful of fresh flat leaf parsley, chopped
4 fresh or 2 dried bay leaves
2 sprigs of thyme

MAKES ABOUT 1 LITRE

Melt the butter and oil in a large, heavy-based saucepan. Add the garlic, fry for 2 minutes, then add the remaining ingredients. Cook, stirring constantly, until softened but not browned.

Add 3 litres of water and bring to the boil. Reduce the heat, cover and simmer for 1½ hours. Let cool.

Return the pan to the heat and simmer for 15 minutes. Strain the stock and return to the pan. Discard the solids. Boil rapidly until reduced by half, then use as needed or let cool and keep in the fridge for up to 3 days.

Risotto with Four Cheeses

RISOTTO AI QUATTRO FORMAGGI

FONTINA, GORGONZOLA, TALEGGIO AND PARMESAN ARE MY FAVOURITE FOUR CHEESES. TRY MIXING AND MATCHING YOUR OWN SELECTION OF CHEESES, BUT CHOOSE ONES THAT ARE QUITE CREAMY AND HAVE A GOOD FLAVOUR. USE THEM AT ROOM TEMPERATURE FOR MAXIMUM TASTE.

Put the stock in a saucepan. Heat until almost boiling, then reduce the heat until barely simmering to keep it hot.

Heat the butter and oil in a sauté pan or heavy-based casserole over a medium heat. Add the shallots and cook for 1–2 minutes, until softened but not browned. Add the garlic and mix well.

Add the rice and stir, using a wooden spoon, until the grains are well coated and glistening, about 1 minute. Pour in the wine and stir until it has been completely absorbed.

Add 1 ladle of hot stock and simmer, stirring until it has been absorbed. Continue to add the stock at intervals and cook as before, until the liquid has been absorbed and the rice is tender but still firm (*al dente*), about 18–20 minutes. Reserve the last ladle of stock.

Add the reserved stock, the four cheeses, parsley, salt and pepper. Mix well. Remove from the heat, cover and let rest for 2 minutes.

Spoon into warmed bowls, sprinkle with grated Parmesan and serve.

900 ml vegetable stock (page 8)
50 g unsalted butter
1 tablespoon olive oil
8 shallots, finely chopped
1 garlic clove, crushed
275 g risotto rice, such as
    vialone nano, carnaroli or arborio
1 glass white wine, about 125 ml
100 g Parmesan cheese, freshly grated,
    plus extra to serve
50 g Gorgonzola cheese, cut into cubes
50 g Fontina cheese, cut into cubes
50 g Taleggio cheese, rind removed and
    cheese cut into cubes
a handful of fresh flat leaf parsley,
    coarsely chopped
sea salt and freshly ground black pepper

SERVES 4

CHEESE

Risotto with Watercress and Taleggio

RISOTTO AL CRESCIONE E TALEGGIO

TALEGGIO — NAMED AFTER A VALLEY IN BERGAMO WHERE IT ORIGINATES — IS MADE FROM THE MILK OF COWS THAT GRAZE THE ALPINE PASTURES, THEN THE CHEESE IS RIPENED IN CAVES. ITS SWEET FLAVOUR COMPLEMENTS THE PEPPERY TASTE OF WATERCRESS. ROCKET WITH TALEGGIO IS ALSO DELICIOUS.

Put the stock in a saucepan. Heat until almost boiling, then reduce the heat until barely simmering to keep it hot.

Heat two-thirds of the butter and the oil in a sauté pan or heavy-based casserole over a medium heat. Add the shallots and cook for 1–2 minutes, until softened but not browned.

Add the rice and stir, using a wooden spoon, until the grains are well coated and glistening, about 1 minute. Pour in the wine and stir until it has been completely absorbed.

Add 1 ladle of hot stock and simmer, stirring until it has been absorbed. Repeat. After 10 minutes, add the watercress and mix well. Continue to add the stock at intervals and cook as before, for a further 8–10 minutes, until the liquid has been absorbed and the rice is tender but still firm (*al dente*).

Mix in the Parmesan, Taleggio, the remaining butter, salt and pepper. Remove from the heat, cover and let rest for 2 minutes.

Spoon into warmed bowls, top with watercress leaves and serve.

900 ml vegetable stock (page 8)
75 g unsalted butter
1 tablespoon olive oil
8 shallots, finely chopped
275 g risotto rice, such as vialone nano, carnaroli or arborio
½ glass white wine, about 75 ml
a bunch of watercress, trimmed and chopped, plus extra leaves to serve
100 g Parmesan cheese, freshly grated
200 g Taleggio cheese, rind removed and cheese cut into cubes
sea salt and freshly ground black pepper

SERVES 4

Rocket and Blue Cheese Risotto

RISOTTO CON ARUGULA E GORGONZOLA

AGED GORGONZOLA (PICCANTE) IS A HIGHLY AROMATIC AND PUNGENT BLUE-VEINED CHEESE. IF THE FLAVOUR IS TOO STRONG FOR YOUR LIKING, REPLACE IT WITH DOLCELATTE — A YOUNGER, MILDER GORGONZOLA. IF YOU CAN'T FIND WILD ROCKET, USE THE CULTIVATED VARIETY INSTEAD.

Put the stock in a saucepan. Heat until almost boiling, then reduce the heat until barely simmering to keep it hot.

Heat the butter and oil in a sauté pan or heavy-based casserole over a medium heat. Add the shallots and cook for 1–2 minutes, until softened but not browned. Add the garlic and mix well.

Add the rice and stir, using a wooden spoon, until the grains are well coated and glistening, about 1 minute.

Add 1 ladle of hot stock and simmer, stirring until it has been absorbed. Continue to add the stock at intervals and cook as before, until the liquid has been absorbed and the rice is tender but still firm (*al dente*), about 18–20 minutes.

Mix in the rocket, Parmesan, Gorgonzola, salt and pepper. Remove from the heat, cover and let rest for 2 minutes.

Spoon into warmed bowls, drizzle with extra virgin olive oil, if using, and serve immediately.

900 ml vegetable stock (page 8)
50 g unsalted butter
1 tablespoon olive oil
8 shallots, finely chopped
2 garlic cloves, crushed
275 g risotto rice, such as vialone nano, carnaroli or arborio
2 large handfuls of wild rocket leaves
100 g Parmesan cheese, freshly grated
50 g Gorgonzola piccante cheese, cut into cubes
sea salt and freshly ground black pepper
extra virgin olive oil, to serve (optional)

SERVES 4

Saffron Risotto

RISOTTO ALLA MILANESE

THIS CLASSIC RISOTTO IS A SPECIALITY OF LOMBARDY. USE SAFFRON STRANDS RATHER THAN THE POWDERED FORM, WHICH TENDS TO BE OF A LESSER QUALITY AND FLAVOUR. MY SISTERS MAKE THIS DISH OFTEN FOR THEIR FAMILIES AND IT IS PARTICULARLY POPULAR WITH THE CHILDREN.

Put the stock in a saucepan. Heat until almost boiling, then reduce the heat until barely simmering to keep it hot.

Heat the butter and oil in a sauté pan or heavy-based casserole over a medium heat. Add the shallots and cook for 1–2 minutes, until softened but not browned. Add the saffron and stir until the yellow colour is released.

Add the rice and stir, using a wooden spoon, until the grains are well coated and glistening, about 1 minute. Pour in the wine and stir until it has been completely absorbed.

Add 1 ladle of hot stock and simmer, stirring until it has been absorbed. Continue to add the stock at intervals and cook as before, until the liquid has been absorbed and the rice is tender but still firm (*al dente*), about 18–20 minutes. Reserve the last ladle of stock.

Add the reserved stock, Parmesan, cream, parsley, if using, salt and pepper. Mix well. Remove from the heat, cover and let rest for 2 minutes.

Spoon into warmed bowls and serve immediately.

900 ml vegetable stock (page 8)
50 g unsalted butter
1 tablespoon olive oil
8 shallots, finely chopped
½ teaspoon saffron strands
275 g risotto rice, such as vialone nano, carnaroli or arborio
½ glass white wine, about 75 ml
100 g Parmesan cheese, freshly grated
2 tablespoons single cream
a handful of fresh flat leaf parsley, coarsely chopped (optional)
sea salt and freshly ground black pepper

SERVES 4

Risotto with Courgettes and Ricotta
RISOTTO CON ZUCCHINE E RICOTTA

WONDERFUL PRODUCE FROM A LOCAL MARKET IN UMBRIA WAS THE INSPIRATION FOR THIS RISOTTO. SMALL, GARDEN-FRESH COURGETTES AND MILKY WHITE, FLUFFY RICOTTA ARE ESSENTIAL. ITALIAN DELIS AND MOST SUPERMARKETS SELL FRESH RICOTTA.

100 g unsalted butter
4 small courgettes, about 200 g, diced
a handful of fresh mint, leaves torn
a handful of fresh flat leaf parsley, coarsely
    chopped
900 ml vegetable stock (page 8)
1 tablespoon olive oil
8 shallots, finely chopped
2 garlic cloves, crushed
275 g risotto rice, such as vialone nano,
    carnaroli or arborio
1 glass white wine, about 125 ml
100 g fresh ricotta cheese
100 g Parmesan cheese, freshly grated
sea salt and freshly ground black pepper

SERVES 4

Melt half the butter in a frying pan, add the courgettes and cook over a medium heat until tender, about 5 minutes. Add the mint and parsley and mix well. Set aside.

Put the stock in a saucepan. Heat until almost boiling, then reduce the heat until barely simmering to keep it hot.

Heat the remaining butter and the oil in a sauté pan or heavy-based casserole over a medium heat. Add the shallots and cook for 1–2 minutes, until softened but not browned. Add the garlic and mix well.

Add the rice and stir, using a wooden spoon, until the grains are well coated and glistening, about 1 minute. Pour in the wine and stir until it has been completely absorbed.

Add 1 ladle of hot stock and simmer, stirring until the liquid has been absorbed. Continue to add the stock at intervals and cook as before, until all the liquid has been absorbed and the rice is tender but still firm (*al dente*), about 18–20 minutes.

Add the cooked courgettes, ricotta, Parmesan, salt and pepper. Mix well. Remove from the heat, cover and let rest for 2 minutes.

Spoon into warmed bowls and serve immediately.

Barolo Risotto

RISOTTO AL BAROLO

RED WINE RISOTTO IS TRADITIONAL IN MANY GRAPE-GROWING REGIONS IN ITALY. THIS ONE IN PARTICULAR IS FAMOUS. IT IS A SPECIALITY OF PIEDMONT AND IS MADE WITH THE LOCAL BAROLO. IF THIS WINE IS NOT AVAILABLE, CHOOSE ONE THAT IS FULL-BODIED WITH ROBUST, FRUITY FLAVOURS.

Put the stock in a saucepan. Heat until almost boiling, then reduce the heat until barely simmering to keep it hot.

Heat half the butter and the oil in a sauté pan or heavy-based casserole over a medium heat. Add the shallots, carrot and celery and cook for 1–2 minutes, until softened but not browned. Add the garlic and mix well.

Add the rice and stir, using a wooden spoon, until the grains are well coated and glistening, about 1 minute. Pour in half the wine and stir until it has been completely absorbed.

Add 1 ladle of hot stock and simmer, stirring until it has been absorbed. Continue to add the stock at intervals and cook as before, until all the liquid has been absorbed and the rice is tender but still firm (*al dente*), about 18–20 minutes.

Add the remaining wine and butter, the Parmesan and parsley, salt and pepper. Mix well. Remove from the heat, cover and let rest for 2 minutes.

Spoon into warmed bowls and serve immediately.

900 ml vegetable stock (page 8)
100 g unsalted butter
1 tablespoon olive oil
8 shallots, finely chopped
1 carrot, finely chopped
2 celery stalks, finely chopped
1 garlic clove, crushed
275 g risotto rice, such as vialone nano, carnaroli or arborio
4 glasses Barolo wine or full-bodied red wine, about 500 ml
100 g Parmesan cheese, freshly grated
a handful of fresh flat leaf parsley, coarsely chopped
sea salt and freshly ground black pepper

SERVES 4

Rice Balls
SUPPLÌ DI RISO

THESE CHEESE-RICE BALLS, ALSO KNOWN AS *SUPPLÌ AL TELEFONO*, ARE ENJOYED THROUGHOUT ITALY. IN SICILY THEY ARE CALLED *ARANCINI*, MEANING LITTLE ORANGES. THIS IS A GOOD WAY OF USING RISOTTO TO MAKE DELICIOUS PARTY FOOD OR ANTIPASTO. IT'S FUN TOO.

800 ml vegetable stock (page 8)
50 g unsalted butter
275 g risotto rice, such as vialone nano, carnaroli or arborio
175 g mozzarella cheese, cut into small cubes
6 shallots, finely chopped
a handful of mixed fresh herbs, such as parsley, basil and oregano, chopped
finely grated zest of 1 large unwaxed orange
6 tablespoons freshly grated Parmesan cheese
6 tablespoons olive oil, for frying
sea salt and freshly ground black pepper

BREADCRUMB COATING:
1 egg, lightly beaten
50 g fresh breadcrumbs

MAKES 8, SERVES 4

Put the stock in a saucepan. Heat until almost boiling, then reduce the heat until barely simmering to keep it hot.

Melt the butter in a wide saucepan. Add the rice and stir, using a wooden spoon, until the grains are well coated and glistening, about 1 minute. Add 1 ladle of hot stock and simmer, stirring until it has been absorbed. Continue to add the stock at intervals and cook as before, until all the liquid has been absorbed and the rice is tender but still firm (*al dente*), about 18–20 minutes.

Add the mozzarella, shallots, mixed herbs, orange zest, Parmesan, salt and pepper. Mix well. Remove from the heat and let cool. The rice is easier to handle and shape when it is cold.

Using your hands, shape the flavoured rice into 8 balls. Dip each one into the beaten egg and coat well, then roll them in the breadcrumbs, pressing crumbs onto any uncovered area.

Heat the oil in a frying pan, add the rice balls (in batches, if necessary) and cook until golden on all sides, about 8 minutes. Drain well on kitchen paper. Serve hot or cold.

Fontina and Walnut Risotto

RISOTTO CON FONTINA E NOCI

FONTINA IS A MOUNTAIN CHEESE FROM LOMBARDY AND IT IS DELICATELY FLAVOURED — MILD ENOUGH NOT TO OVERPOWER THE WALNUTS. I FIRST HAD THIS COMFORTING RISOTTO ON A COLD BUT BRIGHT WINTRY DAY IN BERGAMO, IN THE NORTH OF ITALY. FONTINA IS ALSO USED IN LASAGNE, *FONDUTA* — A KIND OF FONDUE — OR, AS I LIKE IT, MELTED IN A TOASTED SANDWICH FILLED WITH WILD ROCKET.

900 ml vegetable stock (page 8)
50 g unsalted butter
1 tablespoon olive oil
8 shallots, finely chopped
1 garlic clove, crushed
275 g risotto rice, such as vialone nano,
    carnaroli or arborio
½ glass white wine, about 75 ml
100 g Fontina cheese, cut into cubes
100 g Parmesan cheese, freshly grated
50 g shelled walnuts, coarsely chopped
a handful of fresh flat leaf parsley,
    coarsely chopped
sea salt and freshly ground black pepper

TO SERVE (OPTIONAL):
shelled walnuts, coarsely chopped
freshly grated Parmesan cheese

SERVES 4

Put the stock in a saucepan. Heat until almost boiling, then reduce the heat until barely simmering to keep it hot.

Heat the butter and oil in a sauté pan or heavy-based casserole over a medium heat. Add the shallots and cook for 1–2 minutes, until softened but not browned. Add the garlic and mix well.

Add the rice and stir, using a wooden spoon, until the grains are well coated and glistening, about 1 minute. Pour in the wine and stir until it has been completely absorbed.

Add 1 ladle of hot stock and simmer, stirring until it has been absorbed. Continue to add the stock at intervals and cook as before, until the liquid has been absorbed and the rice is tender but still firm (*al dente*), about 18–20 minutes. Reserve the last ladle of stock.

Add the reserved stock, Fontina, Parmesan, walnuts, parsley, salt and pepper. Stir well. Remove from the heat, cover and let rest for 2 minutes.

Spoon into warmed bowls, sprinkle with walnuts and grated Parmesan, if using, and serve immediately.

Potato, Basil and Green Bean Risotto

RISOTTO ALLA GENOVESE

A CLASSIC RISOTTO FROM GENOA. AT FIRST YOU MIGHT BE ALARMED AT THE COMBINATION OF POTATOES, RICE AND BEANS. DON'T BE, IT'S ABSOLUTELY DELICIOUS AND MAKES A SUBSTANTIAL MEAL. SPOONING FRESH PESTO (HOME-MADE OR STORE-BOUGHT) ON TOP BEFORE SERVING IS OPTIONAL, BUT IF YOU LOVE BASIL, THIS WILL INTENSIFY THE FLAVOUR DRAMATICALLY.

Put the stock in a saucepan. Heat until almost boiling, then reduce the heat until barely simmering to keep it hot.

Heat the butter and oil in a sauté pan or heavy-based casserole over a medium heat. Add the shallots and cook for 1–2 minutes, until softened but not browned. Add the garlic and mix well.

Add the rice and stir, using a wooden spoon, until the grains are well coated and glistening, about 1 minute. Pour in the wine and stir until it has been completely absorbed.

Add the potatoes and beans. Add 1 ladle of hot stock and simmer, stirring until it has been absorbed. Continue to add the stock at intervals and cook as before, until all the liquid has been absorbed and the rice is tender but still firm (*al dente*), about 18–20 minutes.

Add the Parmesan, basil, salt and pepper. Mix well. Remove from the heat, cover and let rest for 2 minutes.

Spoon into warmed bowls, top with basil and drizzle with olive oil or fresh pesto, if using. Serve immediately.

900 ml vegetable stock (page 8)
50 g unsalted butter
1 tablespoon olive oil
8 shallots, finely chopped
2 garlic cloves, crushed
275 g risotto rice, such as vialone nano, carnaroli or arborio
½ glass white wine, about 75 ml
4 medium new potatoes, scrubbed and cut into 1 cm cubes
50 g green beans, cut into 1 cm lengths
100 g Parmesan cheese, freshly grated
a large handful of fresh basil, leaves torn
sea salt and freshly ground black pepper

TO SERVE:
fresh basil leaves
olive oil (optional)
fresh pesto (optional)

SERVES 4

Risotto with Chickpeas and Tomatoes
RISOTTO CON CECI E POMODORI

CHICKPEAS ARE A FAVOURITE IN ITALIAN COOKING, ADDED TO SOUPS, PASTA, RICE AND SALADS. THEY HAVE A NUTTY FLAVOUR, CREAMY TEXTURE AND ARE PACKED WITH ENERGY.

Put the stock in a saucepan. Bring to the boil, then reduce the heat until barely simmering to keep it hot.

Heat the butter and oil in a sauté pan or heavy-based casserole over a medium heat. Add the shallots and cook for 1–2 minutes, until softened but not browned. Add the garlic and mix well.

Add the rice and stir, using a wooden spoon, until the grains are well coated and glistening, about 1 minute. Pour in the wine and stir until it has been completely absorbed.

Add 1 ladle of hot stock and simmer, stirring until it has been absorbed. Continue to add the stock at intervals and cook as before, until the liquid has been absorbed and the rice is tender but still firm (*al dente*), about 18–20 minutes. Reserve the last ladle of stock.

Add the reserved stock, chickpeas, tomatoes, Parmesan, parsley, salt and pepper. Mix well. Remove from the heat, cover and let rest for 2 minutes.

Spoon into warmed bowls and serve immediately.

900 ml vegetable stock (page 8)
50 g unsalted butter
1 tablespoon olive oil
8 shallots, finely chopped
2 garlic cloves, crushed
275 g risotto rice, such as vialone nano, carnaroli or arborio
½ glass white wine, about 75 ml
100 g cooked chickpeas or canned, rinsed and drained
4–6 firm tomatoes, deseeded and chopped
100 g Parmesan cheese, freshly grated
a handful of fresh flat leaf parsley, coarsely chopped
sea salt and freshly ground black pepper

SERVES 4

Risotto with **Beans**
RISOTTO CON FAGIOLI

CANNELLINI BEANS WITH PASTA OR RICE MAKE A MUCH-LOVED MEAL IN ITALY. OTHER BEANS, SUCH AS BORLOTTI OR FLAGEOLETS, ARE ALSO DELICIOUS. USE CARNAROLI RICE IN THIS DISH; IT HAS LESS STARCH THAN OTHER RISOTTO RICE AND A TEXTURE THAT EQUALS THAT OF THE BEANS.

900 ml vegetable stock (page 8)
50 g unsalted butter
2 tablespoons olive oil
8 shallots, finely chopped
2 garlic cloves, crushed
275 g carnaroli rice
½ glass white wine, about 75 ml
250 g cooked cannellini beans or canned, rinsed and drained
4 firm tomatoes, deseeded and chopped
grated zest of 1 unwaxed lemon
100 g Parmesan cheese, freshly grated
a handful of freshly torn basil or finely chopped rosemary
a handful of fresh flat leaf parsley, finely chopped
sea salt and freshly ground black pepper
extra virgin olive oil, to serve (optional)

SERVES 4

Put the stock in a saucepan. Heat until almost boiling, then reduce the heat until barely simmering to keep it hot.

Heat the butter and 1 tablespoon of the oil in a sauté pan or heavy-based casserole over a medium heat. Add the shallots and cook for 1–2 minutes, until softened but not browned. Add the garlic and mix well.

Add the rice and stir, using a wooden spoon, until the grains are well coated and glistening, about 1 minute. Pour in the wine and stir until it has been completely absorbed.

Add 1 ladle of hot stock and simmer, stirring until it has been absorbed. After 10 minutes, add the cannellini beans, tomatoes and lemon zest and mix well. Continue to add the stock at intervals and cook as before, for a further 8–10 minutes, until the liquid has been absorbed and the rice is tender but still firm (*al dente*).

Add the Parmesan, half the herbs, salt and pepper. Stir well. Remove from the heat, cover and let rest for 2 minutes.

Spoon into warmed bowls, sprinkle with the remaining herbs and drizzle with extra virgin olive oil, if using. Serve immediately.

Farmers' Risotto

RISOTTO ALLA CONTADINA

WHEN I CAN'T DECIDE WHAT TO COOK, I OFTEN LOOK TO THE VEGETABLES IN MY FRIDGE FOR INSPIRATION. THEY USUALLY END UP IN A RISOTTO. THIS ONE IS EASY TO MAKE AND YOU CAN USE ANY VEGETABLE YOU LIKE. JUST REMEMBER TO CUT THEM INTO NEAT PIECES FOR EVEN COOKING.

900 ml vegetable stock (page 8)
50 g unsalted butter
1 tablespoon olive oil
8 shallots, finely chopped
1 garlic clove, crushed
275 g risotto rice, such as vialone nano,
　carnaroli or arborio
½ glass white wine, about 75 ml
1 small courgette, finely chopped
2–3 firm tomatoes, deseeded and finely
　chopped
50 g fresh green beans, finely chopped
1 small leek, washed and finely sliced
100 g Parmesan cheese, freshly grated
2 tablespoons single cream
a handful of fresh flat leaf parsley,
　finely chopped
a handful of fresh basil, leaves torn
sea salt and freshly ground black pepper
extra virgin olive oil, to serve (optional)

SERVES 4

Put the stock in a saucepan. Heat until almost boiling, then reduce the heat until barely simmering to keep it hot.

Heat the butter and oil in a sauté pan or heavy-based casserole over a medium heat. Add the shallots and cook for 1–2 minutes, until softened but not browned. Add the garlic and mix well.

Add the rice and stir, using a wooden spoon, until the grains are well coated and glistening, about 1 minute. Pour in the wine and stir until it has been completely absorbed.

Add 1 ladle of hot stock and simmer, stirring until it has been absorbed. Repeat. After 10 minutes, add all the vegetables and mix well. Continue to add stock at intervals and cook as before, for a further 8–10 minutes, until the liquid has been absorbed and the vegetables and rice are tender but still firm (*al dente*).

Mix in the Parmesan, cream, half the herbs, salt and pepper. Remove from the heat, cover and let rest for 2 minutes.

Spoon into warmed bowls, top with the remaining herbs and drizzle with extra virgin olive oil, if using. Serve immediately.

Country-style Risotto

RISOTTO ALL' ORTOLANA

A HEARTY DISH – PERFECT ON A COLD WINTRY EVENING. COOK THE VEGETABLES IN A SEPARATE PAN (TO RETAIN THEIR INDIVIDUAL FLAVOURS AND TEXTURES), THEN ADD THEM TO THE RISOTTO. I LOVE BROCCOLI AND OFTEN USE IT IN THIS RISOTTO IF I CAN'T FIND PUMPKIN.

Put the stock in a saucepan. Heat until almost boiling, then reduce the heat until barely simmering to keep it hot.

To cook the vegetables, heat the olive oil in a frying pan and add the garlic, pumpkin, tomatoes, peas, green beans and courgette. Cook until just tender, about 8 minutes, then remove and set aside.

Heat half the butter and the oil in a sauté pan or heavy-based casserole over a medium heat. Add the shallots, carrot, celery and parsley and cook for 1–2 minutes, until softened but not browned.

Add the rice and stir, using a wooden spoon, until the grains are well coated and glistening, about 1 minute. Pour in the wine and stir until it has been completely absorbed.

Add 1 ladle of hot stock and simmer, stirring until it has been absorbed. Continue to add the stock at intervals and cook as before, until the liquid has been absorbed and the rice is tender but still firm (al dente), about 18–20 minutes. Reserve the last ladle of stock.

Add the reserved stock and cooked vegetables, salt and pepper. Mix well. Stir in the Parmesan and remaining butter. Mix well. Remove from the heat, cover and let rest for 2 minutes.

Spoon into warmed bowls, sprinkle with chopped parsley and serve immediately.

900 ml vegetable stock (page 8)
100 g unsalted butter
1 tablespoon olive oil
8 shallots, finely chopped
1 carrot, finely chopped
2 celery stalks, finely chopped
a handful of fresh flat leaf parsley, finely chopped, plus extra to serve
275 g risotto rice, such as vialone nano, carnaroli or arborio
1 glass white wine, about 125 ml
100 g Parmesan cheese, freshly grated
sea salt and freshly ground black pepper

VEGETABLES:
1 tablespoon olive oil
2 garlic cloves, crushed
100 g pumpkin flesh, diced
2 ripe plum tomatoes, deseeded and coarsely chopped
50 g fresh or frozen shelled peas
10 green beans, cut into 1 cm lengths
1 small courgette, cut into 1 cm cubes

SERVES 4

Broad Bean and Red Onion Risotto

RISOTTO CON FAVE E CIPOLLA ROSSA

BROAD BEANS ARE AT THEIR MOST TENDER WHEN YOUNG AND SMALL. ONCE SHELLED, THEY NEED NO OTHER PREPARATION. ONLY LARGER, OLDER BEANS NEED TO BE BLANCHED FIRST, THEN POPPED OUT OF THEIR TOUGH, GREY OUTER CASING. RED ONIONS ARE SWEETER THAN ORDINARY ONIONS.

900 ml vegetable stock (see page 8)
50 g unsalted butter
1 tablespoon olive oil
8 shallots, finely chopped
2 garlic cloves, crushed
275 g risotto rice, such as vialone nano, carnaroli or arborio
1 glass white wine, about 125 ml
2 red onions, finely chopped
275 g fresh or frozen shelled broad beans
100 g Parmesan cheese, freshly grated
a handful of fresh mint, chopped
sea salt and freshly ground black pepper

SERVES 4

Put the stock in a saucepan. Heat until almost boiling, then reduce the heat until barely simmering to keep it hot.

Heat the butter and oil in a sauté pan or heavy-based casserole over a medium heat. Add the shallots and cook for 1–2 minutes, until softened but not browned. Add the garlic and mix well.

Add the rice and stir, using a wooden spoon, until the grains are well coated and glistening, about 1 minute. Pour in the wine and stir until it has been completely absorbed.

Add 1 ladle of hot stock and simmer, stirring until it has been absorbed. Repeat. After 10 minutes, add the onions and broad beans. Continue to add the stock at intervals and cook as before, until the liquid has been absorbed and the rice is tender but still firm (*al dente*), about 18–20 minutes. Reserve the last ladle of stock.

Add the reserved stock, Parmesan, mint, salt and pepper. Mix well. Remove from the heat, cover and let rest for 2 minutes.

Spoon into warmed bowls and serve immediately.

Risotto with Asparagus, Peas and Basil
RISOTTO CON ASPARAGI, PISELLI E BASILICO

ONE OF MY ALL-TIME FAVOURITE RISOTTOS — SO LIGHT, FRESH AND VIBRANTLY GREEN. IT REMINDS ME OF EARLY SUMMER, WHEN ASPARAGUS AND PEAS GROW IN ABUNDANCE. TRY TO USE VEGETABLES WHEN THEY ARE IN SEASON, SO THAT YOU CAN ENJOY THEM AT THEIR FINEST AND SWEETEST.

900 ml vegetable stock (page 8)
50 g unsalted butter
1 tablespoon olive oil
8 shallots, finely chopped
275 g risotto rice, such as vialone nano, carnaroli or arborio
½ glass white wine, about 75 ml
350 g asparagus, cut into 4 cm lengths
150 g fresh or frozen shelled peas
finely grated zest of 1 unwaxed lemon
100 g Parmesan cheese, freshly grated
a large handful of fresh basil, leaves torn
sea salt and freshly ground black pepper

TO SERVE (OPTIONAL):
fresh basil leaves
freshly grated Parmesan cheese

SERVES 4

Put the stock in a saucepan. Heat until almost boiling, then reduce the heat until barely simmering to keep it hot.

Heat the butter and oil in a sauté pan or heavy-based casserole over a medium heat. Add the shallots and cook for 1–2 minutes, until softened but not browned.

Add the rice and stir, using a wooden spoon, until the grains are well coated and glistening, about 1 minute. Pour in the wine and stir until it has been completely absorbed.

Add 1 ladle of hot stock and simmer, stirring until it has been absorbed. Repeat. After 10 minutes, add the asparagus, peas and lemon zest and mix well. Continue to add the stock at intervals and cook as before, for a further 8–10 minutes, until the liquid has been absorbed and the rice is tender but still firm (*al dente*).

Add the reserved stock, Parmesan, basil, salt and pepper. Mix well. Remove from the heat, cover and let rest for 2 minutes.

Spoon into warmed bowls and top with basil and grated Parmesan, if using. Serve immediately.

VEGETABLES

Mushroom Risotto with Potatoes

RISOTTO AI FUNGHI CON PATATE

MUSHROOM RISOTTO IS ALWAYS POPULAR. PORTOBELLO MUSHROOMS HAVE AN INTENSE FLAVOUR, BUT YOU CAN USE WHATEVER KIND YOU LIKE. FOR A SPECIAL TREAT, USE WILD MUSHROOMS, SUCH AS PORCINI AND CHANTERELLES. I'VE ADDED POTATOES FOR EXTRA FLAVOUR AND TEXTURE.

900 ml vegetable stock (page 8)
50 g unsalted butter
1 tablespoon olive oil
8 shallots, finely chopped
2 garlic cloves, crushed
200 g portobello mushrooms or mixed wild
   mushrooms, cut into chunks if large
4 medium new potatoes, scrubbed and cut
   into small chunks
1 sprig of rosemary, finely chopped
275 g risotto rice, such as vialone nano,
   carnaroli or arborio
½ glass white wine, about 75 ml
100 g Parmesan cheese, freshly grated
2 tablespoons single cream
a handful of fresh flat leaf parsley,
   coarsely chopped, plus extra to serve
sea salt and freshly ground black pepper

SERVES 4

Put the stock in a saucepan. Heat until almost boiling, then reduce the heat until barely simmering to keep it hot.

Heat the butter and oil in a sauté pan or heavy-based casserole over a medium heat. Add the shallots and cook for 1–2 minutes, until softened but not browned. Add the garlic, mushrooms, potatoes and rosemary. Mix well.

Add the rice and stir, using a wooden spoon, until the grains are well coated and glistening, about 1 minute. Pour in the wine and stir until it has been completely absorbed.

Add 1 ladle of hot stock and simmer, stirring until it has been absorbed. Continue to add the stock at intervals and cook as before, until the liquid has been absorbed and the rice is tender but still firm (*al dente*), about 18–20 minutes. Reserve the last ladle of stock.

Add the reserved stock, Parmesan, cream, parsley, salt and pepper. Mix well. Remove from the heat, cover and let rest for 2 minutes.

Spoon into warmed bowls, sprinkle with chopped parsley and serve immediately.

Pumpkin Risotto

RISOTTO DI ZUCCA

A GREAT FAVOURITE IN NORTHERN ITALY. I ADORE PUMPKIN AND IN ITALY IT IS EATEN ALL YEAR ROUND, NOT JUST IN AUTUMN. IT IS USED IN ENDLESS WAYS — SWEET AND SAVOURY — FROM SOUPS TO STEWS AND FROM PASTA FILLINGS TO FLAVOURED BREADS AND CAKES. PUMPKINS VARY ENORMOUSLY — THE BEST ONE TO USE IS THE ORANGE-FLESHED, SLIGHTLY SWEET VARIETY.

Put the stock in a saucepan. Heat until almost boiling, then reduce the heat until barely simmering to keep it hot.

Heat the butter and oil in a sauté pan or heavy-based casserole over a medium heat. Add the shallots and cook for 1–2 minutes, until softened but not browned. Add the garlic and mix well.

Add the rice and stir, using a wooden spoon, until the grains are well coated and glistening, about 1 minute. Pour in the wine and stir until it has been completely absorbed.

Add 1 ladle of hot stock, the pumpkin or butternut and parsley. Simmer, stirring until the liquid has been absorbed. Continue to add the stock at intervals and cook as before, until the liquid has been absorbed, the pumpkin is cooked and the rice is tender but firm (al dente), about 18–20 minutes. Reserve the last ladle of stock.

Add the reserved stock, Parmesan, salt and pepper. Mix well. Remove from the heat, cover and let rest for 2 minutes.

Spoon into warmed bowls and serve immediately.

900 ml vegetable stock (page 8)
50 g unsalted butter
1 tablespoon olive oil
8 shallots, finely chopped
2 garlic cloves, crushed
275 g risotto rice, such as vialone nano, carnaroli or arborio
1 glass white wine, about 125 ml
400 g pumpkin or butternut squash, peeled, deseeded and cut into 1 cm cubes
a handful of fresh flat leaf parsley, coarsely chopped
100 g Parmesan cheese, freshly grated
sea salt and freshly ground black pepper

SERVES 4

Tomato Risotto

RISOTTO AL POMODORO

I LIKE THE SIMPLICITY OF THIS DISH — THIS IS PROBABLY WHY IT'S POPULAR WITH CHILDREN AS WELL AS GROWN-UPS. IT'S ALMOST IMPOSSIBLE TO IMAGINE ITALIAN FOOD WITHOUT TOMATOES — USE A FULL-FLAVOURED VARIETY, FIRM, RED AND WITH A GOOD FRUITY SCENT.

900 ml vegetable stock (page 8)
50 g unsalted butter
1 tablespoon olive oil
8 shallots, finely chopped
2 garlic cloves, crushed
275 g risotto rice, such as vialone nano, carnaroli or arborio
½ glass white wine, about 75 ml
8 firm tomatoes, deseeded and coarsely chopped
100 g Parmesan cheese, freshly grated, plus extra to serve
a large handful of fresh basil, leaves torn
sea salt and freshly ground black pepper

SERVES 4

Put the stock in a saucepan. Heat until almost boiling, then reduce the heat until barely simmering to keep it hot.

Heat the butter and oil in a sauté pan or heavy-based casserole over a medium heat. Add the shallots and cook for 1–2 minutes, until softened but not browned. Add the garlic and mix well.

Add the rice and stir, using a wooden spoon, until the grains are well coated and glistening, about 1 minute. Pour in the wine and stir until it has been completely absorbed.

Add 1 ladle of hot stock and simmer, stirring until it has been absorbed. Repeat. After 10 minutes, add the tomatoes. Continue to add the stock at intervals and cook as before, for a further 8–10 minutes, until the liquid has been absorbed and the tomatoes and rice are tender but still firm (al dente). Reserve the last ladle of stock.

Add the reserved stock, Parmesan, basil, salt and pepper. Mix well. Remove from the heat, cover and let rest for 2 minutes.

Spoon into warmed bowls, sprinkle with grated Parmesan and serve immediately.

Radicchio Risotto

RISOTTO AL RADICCHIO

MADDALENA CHEPELLO — A FAMILY FRIEND — TAUGHT ME HOW TO COOK THIS COLOURFUL VEGETABLE. THERE ARE TWO VARIETIES; ROUND AND LONG (TREVISO). USE TREVISO IF YOU CAN — IT IS LESS BITTER AND HAS MORE FLAVOUR. MY FATHER GROWS RADICCHIO, SO I HAVE A SPECIAL FONDNESS FOR IT.

900 ml vegetable stock (page 8)
50 g unsalted butter
1 tablespoon olive oil
8 shallots, finely chopped
275 g risotto rice, such as vialone nano,
   carnaroli or arborio
½ glass white wine, about 75 ml
2 medium radicchio, preferably Treviso,
   finely sliced
100 g Parmesan cheese, freshly grated, plus
   extra to serve
2 tablespoons single cream
a handful of fresh basil, leaves torn
sea salt and freshly ground black pepper

SERVES 4

Put the stock in a saucepan. Heat until almost boiling, then reduce the heat until barely simmering to keep it hot.

Heat the butter and oil in a sauté pan or heavy-based casserole over a medium heat. Add the shallots and cook for 1–2 minutes, until softened but not browned.

Add the rice and stir, using a wooden spoon, until the grains are well coated and glistening, about 1 minute. Pour in the wine and stir until it has been completely absorbed.

Add 1 ladle of hot stock and simmer, stirring until it has been absorbed. Repeat. After 10 minutes, add the radicchio. Continue to add the stock at intervals and cook as before, for a further 8–10 minutes, until the liquid has been absorbed and the rice is tender but still firm (*al dente*). Reserve the last ladle of stock.

Add the reserved stock, Parmesan, cream, basil, salt and pepper. Mix well. Remove from the heat, cover and let rest for 2 minutes.

Spoon into warmed bowls, sprinkle with grated Parmesan and serve.

Risotto with Sage and Leeks
RISOTTO CON SALVIA E PORRI

SAGE IS A PUNGENT HERB, SAID TO HAVE MEMORY-ENHANCING PROPERTIES. ADD LESS SAGE IF YOU FIND IT TOO OVERPOWERING. YOUNG AND TENDER LEEKS HAVE THE MOST FLAVOUR – WASH THEM WELL TO GET RID OF ANY SOIL TRAPPED BETWEEN THE TIGHTLY PACKED LEAVES.

900 ml vegetable stock (page 8)
50 g unsalted butter
1 tablespoon olive oil
8 shallots, finely chopped
a handful of fresh sage, finely chopped
1 garlic clove, crushed
275 g risotto rice, such as vialone nano, carnaroli or arborio
1 glass white wine, about 125 ml
6 baby leeks, washed and finely chopped*
100 g Parmesan cheese, freshly grated
2 tablespoons single cream
sea salt and freshly ground black pepper
4 sage leaves, to serve

SERVES 4

Put the stock in a saucepan. Heat until almost boiling, then reduce the heat until barely simmering to keep it hot.

Heat the butter and oil in a sauté pan or heavy-based casserole over a medium heat. Add the shallots and sage and cook for 2–3 minutes, until softened and lightly golden. Add the garlic.

Add the rice and stir, using a wooden spoon, until the grains are well coated and glistening, about 1 minute. Pour in the wine, stir until it has been completely absorbed, then add the leeks. Mix well.

Add 1 ladle of hot stock and simmer, stirring until it has been absorbed. Continue to add the stock at intervals and cook as before, until the liquid has been absorbed and the rice is tender but still firm (*al dente*), about 18–20 minutes. Reserve the last ladle of stock.

Add the reserved stock, Parmesan, cream, salt and pepper. Mix well. Remove from the heat, cover and let rest for 2 minutes.

Spoon into warmed bowls, top with a sage leaf and serve.

*Note: To clean leeks, cut them in half or quarters down the middle and rinse, shaking them under running water, to dislodge any trapped dirt.

Fennel Risotto

RISOTTO AL FINOCCHIO

WE ITALIANS LOVE FENNEL AND EAT IT BOTH RAW AND COOKED. IT HAS A DISTINCTIVE, ANISEED-LIKE FLAVOUR. TO CLEANSE THE PALATE AFTER A LARGE MEAL, WE EAT IT RAW AS A DIGESTIVE, SO WE CAN CONTINUE TO EAT EVEN MORE. TRY IT — IT WORKS.

Wash and trim the fennel, removing all the hard external green bits. Cut off and reserve the green fronds. Finely slice the fennel.

Put the stock in a saucepan. Heat until almost boiling, then reduce the heat until barely simmering to keep it hot.

Heat the butter and oil in a sauté pan or heavy-based casserole over a medium heat. Add the shallots and cook for 1–2 minutes, until softened but not browned. Add the fennel and lemon zest.

Add the rice and stir, using a wooden spoon, until the grains are well coated and glistening, about 1 minute. Pour in the wine and stir until it has been completely absorbed.

Add 1 ladle of hot stock and simmer, stirring until it has been absorbed. Continue to add the stock at intervals and cook as before, until the liquid has been absorbed and the rice is tender but still firm (*al dente*), about 18–20 minutes. Reserve the last ladle of stock.

Add the reserved stock, Parmesan, cream, salt and pepper. Mix well. Remove from the heat, cover and let rest for 2 minutes.

Spoon into warmed bowls, top with the reserved fennel fronds and serve.

2 medium fennel bulbs with green fronds
900 ml vegetable stock (page 8)
50 g unsalted butter
1 tablespoon olive oil
8 shallots, finely chopped
finely grated zest of 2 unwaxed lemons
275 g risotto rice, such as vialone nano, carnaroli or arborio
½ glass white wine, about 75 ml
100 g Parmesan cheese, freshly grated
2 tablespoons single cream
sea salt and freshly ground black pepper

SERVES 4

Chestnut Risotto

RISOTTO DI CASTAGNE

IN ITALY, THE SEASON FOR CHESTNUTS IS VERY SHORT: FROM THE BEGINNING OF NOVEMBER TO MID

DECEMBER. FRESH CHESTNUTS HAVE A WONDERFUL NUTTY FLAVOUR, BUT IF THEY'RE NOT IN SEASON OR

YOU DON'T HAVE TIME TO PREPARE THEM, USE THE PRE-COOKED, VACUUM-PACKED VARIETY INSTEAD.

250 g fresh chestnuts or 200 g vacuum-
packed, cooked and peeled chestnuts
900 ml vegetable stock (page 8)
50 g unsalted butter
1 tablespoon olive oil
8 shallots, finely chopped
1 garlic clove, crushed
275 g risotto rice, such as vialone nano,
carnaroli or arborio
½ glass white wine, about 75 ml
100 g Parmesan cheese, freshly grated, plus
extra to serve
a handful of fresh flat leaf parsley,
coarsely chopped
sea salt and freshly ground black pepper

SERVES 4

If using fresh chestnuts, cut a cross in the blunt end of each one,
then put in a roasting tin and cook in a preheated oven at 180°C
(350°F) Gas 4 for 25–30 minutes or until they split open. Let cool,
then peel. Coarsely chop the chestnuts.

Put the stock in a saucepan. Heat until almost boiling, then reduce
the heat until barely simmering to keep it hot.

Heat the butter and oil in a sauté pan or heavy-based casserole
over a medium heat. Add the shallots and cook for 1–2 minutes,
until softened but not browned. Add the garlic and mix well.

Add the rice and stir, using a wooden spoon, until the grains are
well coated and glistening, about 1 minute. Pour in the wine and
stir until it has been completely absorbed.

Add 1 ladle of hot stock and simmer, stirring until it has been
absorbed. Repeat. After about 10 minutes, add the chestnuts and
mix well. Continue to add the stock at intervals and cook as before,
for a further 8–10 minutes, until the liquid has been absorbed and
the rice is tender but still firm (*al dente*).

Add the Parmesan, parsley, salt and pepper. Mix well. Remove
from the heat, cover and let rest for 2 minutes.

Spoon into warmed bowls and serve with grated Parmesan.

Risotto with Truffles
RISOTTO AL TARTUFO

TRUFFLES ARE SYNONYMOUS WITH ITALY AND ARE A REAL LUXURY. IF YOU ARE LUCKY ENOUGH TO HAVE ONE, SHAVE IT FINELY OVER THE RISOTTO. IF YOU DON'T, AN EXTRA SPOONFUL OF TRUFFLE OIL WILL REMIND YOU OF WHAT YOU'RE MISSING. STORE TRUFFLES IN AN AIRTIGHT JAR OF RISOTTO RICE.

Put the stock in a saucepan. Heat until almost boiling, then reduce the heat until barely simmering to keep it hot.

Heat the butter and oil in a sauté pan or heavy-based casserole over a medium heat. Add the shallots and cook for 1–2 minutes, until softened but not browned.

Add the rice and stir, using a wooden spoon, until the grains are well coated and glistening, about 1 minute. Pour in the wine and stir until it has been completely absorbed.

Add 1 ladle of hot stock and simmer, stirring until it has been absorbed. Continue to add the stock at intervals and cook as before, until the liquid has been absorbed and the rice is tender but firm (al dente), about 18–20 minutes. Reserve the last ladle of stock.

Add the reserved stock, Parmesan, cream, truffle oil, parsley, salt and pepper. Mix well. Remove from the heat, cover and let rest for 2 minutes.

Spoon into warmed bowls and shave paper-thin slices of truffle over the top, if using. Serve immediately.

900 ml vegetable stock (page 8)
50 g unsalted butter
1 tablespoon olive oil
8 shallots, finely chopped
275 g risotto rice, such as vialone nano, carnaroli or arborio
½ glass white wine, about 75 ml
100 g Parmesan cheese, freshly grated
2 tablespoons single cream
2 tablespoons truffle oil
a handful of fresh flat leaf parsley, coarsely chopped
sea salt and freshly ground black pepper
1 fresh black or white truffle, to serve (optional)

SERVES 4

Risotto with Lemon and Mint

RISOTTO CON LIMONE E MENTA

MOST COOKS WILL HAVE A COUPLE OF LEMONS IN THE KITCHEN AND MINT GROWING IN THE GARDEN, SO THIS RISOTTO NEEDS LITTLE PLANNING OR FORETHOUGHT. IT'S IDEAL FOR AN IMPROMPTU MEAL WHEN FRIENDS VISIT OR IF YOU WANT A DELICIOUS SUPPER WITHOUT HASSLE.

900 ml vegetable stock (page 8)
50 g unsalted butter
1 tablespoon olive oil
8 shallots, finely chopped
1 garlic clove, crushed
275 g risotto rice, such as vialone nano,
   carnaroli or arborio
½ glass white wine, about 75 ml
100 g Parmesan cheese, freshly grated
finely grated zest of 3 unwaxed lemons
2 tablespoons single cream
a handful of fresh mint, coarsely chopped
sea salt and freshly ground black pepper

TO SERVE:
chopped fresh mint
extra virgin olive oil

SERVES 4

Put the stock in a saucepan. Heat until almost boiling, then reduce the heat until barely simmering to keep it hot.

Heat the butter and oil in a sauté pan or heavy-based casserole over a medium heat. Add the shallots and cook for 1–2 minutes, until softened but not browned. Add the garlic and mix well.

Add the rice and stir, using a wooden spoon, until the grains are well coated and glistening, about 1 minute. Pour in the wine and stir until it has been completely absorbed.

Add 1 ladle of hot stock and simmer, stirring until it has been absorbed. Continue to add the stock at intervals and cook as before, until the liquid has been absorbed and the rice is tender but firm (*al dente*), about 18–20 minutes.

Add the Parmesan, lemon zest, cream, mint, salt and pepper. Mix well. Remove from the heat, cover and let rest for 2 minutes.

Spoon into warmed bowls, top with chopped mint and drizzle with extra virgin olive oil. Serve immediately.

Risotto with Olives and Red Peppers

RISOTTO CON OLIVE E PEPERONI ROSSI

A ROBUST RISOTTO, RICH WITH MEDITERRANEAN FLAVOURS. USE OLIVES WHICH HAVE BEEN PITTED AND MARINATED WITH HERBS AND GARLIC, AVAILABLE FROM ITALIAN DELIS. DON'T USE THE CANNED VARIETY. ROASTING PEPPERS CONCENTRATES THEIR FLAVOUR BY CARAMELIZING THEIR NATURAL JUICES.

Roast the peppers in a preheated oven at 200°C (400°F) Gas 6 for 15–20 minutes, until blistered and charred. Seal in a plastic bag for 10 minutes, then scrape off the skin. Cut the peppers in half and remove and discard the seeds. Cut the flesh into squares. Set aside.

Put the stock in a saucepan. Heat until almost boiling, then reduce the heat until barely simmering to keep it hot.

Heat the butter and oil in a sauté pan or heavy-based casserole over a medium heat. Add the shallots and cook for 1–2 minutes, until softened but not browned. Add the garlic and mix well.

Add the rice and stir, using a wooden spoon, until the grains are well coated and glistening, about 1 minute. Pour in the wine and stir until it has been completely absorbed.

Add 1 ladle of hot stock and simmer, stirring until it has been absorbed. Continue to add the stock at intervals and cook as before, until the liquid has been absorbed and the rice is tender but still firm (*al dente*), about 18–20 minutes. Reserve the last ladle of stock.

Add the reserved stock and roasted peppers, the Parmesan, olives, parsley, salt and pepper. Mix well. Remove from the heat, cover and let rest for 2 minutes.

Spoon into warmed bowls, sprinkle with chopped parsley and serve immediately.

2 medium red peppers
900 ml vegetable stock (page 8)
50 g unsalted butter
1 tablespoon olive oil
8 shallots, finely chopped
2 garlic cloves, crushed
275 g risotto rice, such as vialone nano, carnaroli or arborio
½ glass white wine, about 75 ml
100 g Parmesan cheese, freshly grated
50 g black olives, about 10, pitted and coarsely chopped
a handful of fresh flat leaf parsley, coarsely chopped, plus extra to serve
sea salt and freshly ground black pepper

SERVES 4

Risotto with
Mushrooms, Cognac and Cream
RISOTTO CON FUNGHI, COGNAC E PANNA

I LOVE TRADITIONAL ITALIAN FOOD, SO WHEN MY FRIEND INTRODUCED ME TO THIS VERY MODERN RISOTTO I WAS PLEASANTLY SURPRISED AT HOW MUCH I LIKED IT. WE ATE THIS RICH, CREAMY RISOTTO AT PECK – A WONDERFUL RESTAURANT IN MILAN. THIS DISH IS SUBSTANTIAL AS WELL AS COMFORTING.

Heat half the butter in a frying pan until foaming, then add the mushrooms and cook for 5 minutes. Add salt and pepper. Add the Cognac or brandy, boil until reduced by half, then stir in the cream. Simmer for 5 minutes, until the sauce has thickened slightly. Set aside.

Put the stock in a saucepan. Heat until almost boiling, then reduce the heat until barely simmering to keep it hot.

Heat the remaining butter and oil in a sauté pan or heavy-based casserole over a medium heat. Add the shallots and cook for 1–2 minutes, until softened but not browned. Add the garlic.

Add the rice and stir, using a wooden spoon, until the grains are well coated and glistening, about 1 minute.

Add 1 ladle of hot stock and simmer, stirring until it has been absorbed. Continue to add the stock at intervals and cook as before, until the liquid has been absorbed and the rice is tender but firm (al dente), about 18–20 minutes.

Add the reserved mushroom mixture, the grated Parmesan, parsley, salt and pepper. Mix well. Remove from the heat, cover and let rest for 2 minutes.

Spoon into warmed bowls, top with Parmesan shavings and serve.

100 g unsalted butter
275 g large, open-cap mushrooms, finely sliced
1 tablespoon Cognac or other brandy
3 tablespoons single cream
900 ml vegetable stock (page 8)
1 tablespoon olive oil
8 shallots, finely chopped
2 garlic cloves, crushed
275 g risotto rice, such as vialone nano, carnaroli or arborio
100 g Parmesan cheese, freshly grated
a handful of fresh flat leaf parsley, coarsely chopped
sea salt and freshly ground black pepper
shavings of Parmesan cheese, to serve

SERVES 4

Risotto with Seven Wild Herbs

RISOTTO CON SETTE ERBE SELVATICHE

THIS RISOTTO CAME ABOUT BY ACCIDENT. I HAD PICKED SOME WILD HERBS FROM MY GARDEN IN ITALY AND COULDN'T DECIDE WHICH TO USE TO FLAVOUR MY RISOTTO, SO I ADDED THEM ALL. THE RESULT WAS FANTASTIC. USE MY SUGGESTION OF HERBS OR CHOOSE YOUR OWN. YOU DON'T EVEN HAVE TO USE SEVEN HERBS, ALTHOUGH IN ITALY THIS NUMBER IS BELIEVED TO BRING GOOD LUCK.

Put the stock in a saucepan. Heat until almost boiling, then reduce the heat until barely simmering to keep it hot.

Heat the butter and oil in a sauté pan or heavy-based casserole over a medium heat. Add the shallots and cook for 1–2 minutes, until softened but not browned.

Add the rice and stir, using a wooden spoon, until the grains are well coated and glistening, about 1 minute. Pour in the wine and stir until it has been completely absorbed.

Add 1 ladle of hot stock and simmer, stirring until it has been absorbed. Continue to add the stock at intervals and cook as before, until the liquid has been absorbed and the rice is tender but firm (*al dente*), about 18–20 minutes. Reserve the last ladle of stock.

Add the reserved stock, Parmesan, cream, mixed herbs, salt and pepper. Mix well. Remove from the heat, cover and let rest for 2 minutes.

Spoon into warmed bowls, sprinkle with chopped mixed herbs and serve immediately.

900 ml vegetable stock (page 8)
50 g unsalted butter
1 tablespoon olive oil
8 shallots, finely chopped
275 g risotto rice, such as vialone nano, carnaroli or arborio
½ glass white wine, about 75 ml
100 g Parmesan cheese, freshly grated
2 tablespoons single cream
a handful of mixed fresh herbs, such as sage, parsley, basil, thyme, mint, oregano and marjoram, chopped, plus extra to serve
sea salt and freshly ground black pepper

SERVES 4

Risotto with

Aubergine, Pine Nuts and Tomatoes

RISOTTO CON MELANZANE, PINOLI E POMODORI

I FIRST TASTED THIS DISH IN A TINY TRATTORIA IN ROME, ONE BALMY EVENING IN LATE SUMMER. IT ALWAYS REMINDS ME OF BEING IN ITALY. SALTING THE AUBERGINES BEFORE COOKING WILL REMOVE ANY BITTERNESS AND TOASTING THE PINE NUTS UNTIL GOLDEN WILL INTENSIFY THEIR NUTTY FLAVOUR.

1 small aubergine, about 200 g, diced
3 tablespoons olive oil
4–6 firm tomatoes, deseeded and chopped
900 ml vegetable stock (page 8)
50 g unsalted butter
8 shallots, finely chopped
2 garlic cloves, crushed
275 g risotto rice, such as vialone nano,
   carnaroli or arborio
1 glass white wine, about 125 ml
100 g Parmesan cheese, freshly grated
50 g pine nuts, pan-toasted
a handful of fresh flat leaf parsley,
   coarsely chopped
a handful of fresh basil, coarsely chopped
sea salt and freshly ground black pepper

SERVES 4

Put the aubergine in a colander set over a bowl. Sprinkle with salt and let stand for 10–15 minutes. Rinse to remove the salt and pat dry. Heat 2 tablespoons of the oil in a frying pan, add the aubergine and cook until golden. Add the tomatoes and cook until softened.

Put the stock in a saucepan. Heat until almost boiling, then reduce the heat until barely simmering to keep it hot.

Heat the butter and remaining oil in a sauté pan or heavy-based casserole over a medium heat. Add the shallots and cook for 1–2 minutes, until softened but not browned. Add the garlic.

Add the rice and stir, using a wooden spoon, until the grains are well coated and glistening, about 1 minute. Pour in the wine and stir until it has been completely absorbed.

Add 1 ladle of hot stock and simmer, stirring until it has been absorbed. Continue to add the stock at intervals and cook as before, until the liquid has been absorbed and the rice is tender but firm (al dente), about 18–20 minutes. Reserve the last ladle of stock.

Add the reserved stock, the aubergine and tomato mixture, the Parmesan, pine nuts, parsley, basil, salt and pepper. Mix well. Remove from the heat, cover and let rest for 2 minutes.

Spoon into warmed bowls and serve immediately.

Artichoke Risotto

RISOTTO CON I CARCIOFI

TRY TO BUY YOUNG ARTICHOKES WITH LONG, UNCUT STEMS. THE SHORTER THE STEM, THE

TOUGHER THE ARTICHOKE TENDS TO BE. YOUNG ARTICHOKES ARE ALSO LESS FIBROUS. FIRMLY

CLOSED ARTICHOKES ARE AN INDICATION OF FRESHNESS; IF THE LEAVES ARE OPEN THEY ARE OLD.

To prepare the artichokes, pull off the tough outer leaves and cut off the spiky, pointed top. Remove the stalk and cut each artichoke lengthways into 4 segments if small or 8 segments if large. Cut away the fuzzy, prickly choke. Squeeze the lemon over the segments to prevent discoloration. Set aside.

Put the stock in a saucepan. Heat until almost boiling, then reduce the heat until barely simmering to keep it hot.

Heat the butter and oil in a sauté pan or heavy-based casserole over a medium heat. Add the shallots and cook for 1–2 minutes, until softened but not browned. Add the garlic and artichoke segments and cook for 2–3 minutes.

Add the rice and stir, using a wooden spoon, until the grains are well coated and glistening, about 1 minute. Pour in the wine and stir until it has been completely absorbed.

Add 1 ladle of hot stock and simmer, stirring until it has been absorbed. Continue to add the stock at intervals and cook as before, until the liquid has been absorbed and the rice is tender but firm (*al dente*), about 18–20 minutes.

Add the Parmesan, mascarpone, parsley, salt and pepper. Mix well. Remove from the heat, cover and let rest for 2 minutes.

Spoon into warmed bowls and serve with grated Parmesan.

4 small or 2 large globe artichokes
1 lemon, halved
900 ml vegetable stock (page 8)
50 g unsalted butter
1 tablespoon olive oil
8 shallots, finely chopped
1 garlic clove, crushed
275 g risotto rice, such as vialone nano, carnaroli or arborio
½ glass white wine, about 75 ml
100 g Parmesan cheese, freshly grated, plus extra to serve
2 tablespoons mascarpone cheese
a handful of fresh flat leaf parsley, coarsely chopped
sea salt and freshly ground black pepper

SERVES 4

Broccoli and Lemon Risotto

RISOTTO CON BROCCOLETTI E LIMONE

I WAS SERVED THIS RISOTTO IN SANT' AMBROGIO — A RESTAURANT NAMED AFTER THE PATRON SAINT OF MILAN. PURPLE SPROUTING BROCCOLI HAS A DELICIOUS NUTTY FLAVOUR, BUT IF YOU CAN'T FIND IT USE BROCCOLI INSTEAD.

900 ml vegetable stock (page 8)
50 g unsalted butter
1 tablespoon olive oil
8 shallots, finely chopped
2 garlic cloves, crushed
275 g risotto rice, such as vialone nano,
    carnaroli or arborio
1 glass white wine, about 125 ml
275 g purple sprouting broccoli or broccoli
    florets
100 g Parmesan cheese, freshly grated
finely grated zest of 2 unwaxed lemons
a handful of fresh flat leaf parsley,
    coarsely chopped, plus extra to serve
sea salt and freshly ground black pepper

SERVES 4

Put the stock in a saucepan. Heat until almost boiling, then reduce the heat until barely simmering to keep it hot.

Heat the butter and oil in a sauté pan or heavy-based casserole over a medium heat. Add the shallots and cook for 1–2 minutes, until softened but not browned. Add the garlic and mix well.

Add the rice and stir, using a wooden spoon, until the grains are well coated and glistening, about 1 minute. Pour in the wine and stir until it has been completely absorbed.

Add 1 ladle of hot stock and simmer, stirring until it has been absorbed. Repeat. After 10 minutes, add the broccoli. Continue to add the stock at intervals and cook as before, for a further 8–10 minutes, until the liquid has been absorbed and the broccoli and rice are tender but still firm (al dente).

Add the Parmesan, lemon zest, parsley, salt and pepper. Mix well. Remove from the heat, cover and let rest for 2 minutes.

Spoon into warmed bowls, sprinkle with chopped parsley and serve immediately.

index